Copyright © 2017 by Josh Graf

All rights reserved. No part of this publication may be reproduced, distributed, or transmitted in any form or by any means, including photocopying, recording, or other electronic or mechanical methods, without the prior written permission of the publisher, except in the case of brief quotations embodied in critical reviews and certain other noncommercial uses permitted by copyright law.

THE BEST OF THE WORST

DAD JOKES

BY: JOSH GRAF

INTRODUCTION

What is a dad joke? There are five steps to a good dad joke.

1. Make it short.
2. Have good timing.
3. Make it punny or silly.
4. Make sure you're a dad.
5. Deliver it with a smile.

Of course, there are exceptions to every rule, but if you need some practice or need a few starting jokes, these best of the worst dad jokes are for you.

Why can't you play jokes on snakes?

Because you can't pull their legs.

Why are pigs so bad at basketball?

They always hog the ball.

What kind of plane does the pope like to fly in?

A holy-copter.

Why was the baby strawberry crying?

Because his mom and dad were in a jam.

Why did John walk backwards to school?

It was back to school day.

What did the buffalo say to his son when he left for college?

Bison.

What's a bird's favorite dessert?

Chocolate chirp cookies.

How do you serve a smart hamburger?

On an honor roll.

Why couldn't the pony sing his favorite song?

He was a little hoarse.

Why did the portobellos grow so close together?

They don't need mushroom.

Where does a rabbit learn how to fly?

In the Hare Force.

What kind of animal is always found at baseball games?

A bat.

> Why did the bubble gum cross the road?

> It was stuck to the chicken's foot.

Why is it dangerous to play cards in the jungle?

Because of all the cheetahs.

> What did one eye say to the other eye?

> Don't look now, but something between us smells.

What did the pencil say to the other pencil?

You're lookin' sharp!

Why didn't the skeleton go to the dance?

Because he had no body to go with.

What did the penny say to the other penny?

We make perfect cents.

How can you tell if a vampire has a horrible cold?

By his horrible coffin.

What do you call an alligator that steals?

A crookodile.

What do you call a dinosaur in a car accident?

A tyrannosauraus wreck!

What did the spider do on the computer?

Made a website.

What did the big chimney say to the little chimney?

You're too young to smoke.

Why did the shoelace get in trouble?

Because it was being knotty.

How does a lion greet other animals in wild?

Pleased to eat you.

What do you call a piece of wood with nothing to do?

Board.

What does a cat like to eat on a hot summer's day?

A mice cream cone.

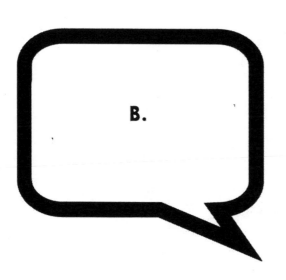

Why did the ice cream cone take boxing lessons?

It was tired of getting licked.

What types of songs do planets sing?

Nep-tunes.

Why did the girl sit on the ladder to sing?

She wanted to hit the high notes.

What did the boy octopus say to the girl octopus?

I want to hold your hand hand hand hand hand hand hand hand.

How do skunks keep in touch with each other?

With their smell phones.

What do bees do if they want to use public transportation?

Go to the buzz stop.

What do pigs get when they have a rash?

Oinkment.

How much does a pirate pay for corn?

A buck an ear.

What do you call a very popular perfume?

A best smeller.

Why do vampires brush their teeth?

To stop bat breath.

Why does the Mississippi river see so well?

Because it has four eyes.

What did the horse say when he fell?

Help, I've fallen and I can't giddy up!

Who do you change a pumpkin into another food?

You throw it up in the air and then it lands as squash.

What do alligators drink after they exercise?

Gator-aid.

Why did the moose head to the gym?

He wanted bigger moosles.

Why wouldn't the shrimp share his treasure?

Because he was a little shellfish.

What do you call a fat pumpkin?

A plumpkin.

Why shouldn't you insult a cat lover?

You'll hurt her felines.

What's a cannibal's favorite game?

Swallow the leader.

Why did the lifeguard get a ticket?

He was caught diving without a license.

Why do bananas wear suntan lotion?

Because they peel.

Why do bees have sticky hair?

Because they use honey combs.

What musical instrument do you find in the bathroom?

A tuba toothpaste.

How do you make a tissue dance?

You put a little boogey in it!

Made in the USA
Columbia, SC
03 December 2017